This book is for YOU!

The Mosquito & The Bumble Bee

by Scot Sax

Written by Scot Sax
Illustrated by Molly Reynolds

Library of Congress Control Number: 2016921317

ISBN 978-0-9985132-0-1

DEDICATION

This book is dedicated
to my wife Suzie,
and our daughters,
Josephine and Chloe.
May our girls always see
the good in everyone,
just like the Mosquito
and the Bumble Bee.

♥

Some say the Mosquito
got evil on her mind.
Spends her days ruining
a perfectly good time.

Just when she sees
happy moonlit faces
she sneaks up and bites them
in hard-to-reach places.

She loves
to watch
them squirm.

She loves
to see
them twitch.

3

She smiles
when they
scratch.

She's tickled
pink when
they itch.

In a black and yellow suit
I see...
Ms. Mosquito's arch rival
Mr. Bumble Bee!

When it comes to ending fun
Mr. Bee is King.
He turns a picnic into chaos
with just one sting.

One pleasant afternoon
in the hills of Stowe
Mr. Bumble Bee came face-to-face
with Ms. Mosquito!

Both had heard
of each other it seems.
Word tends to get around
like fishes in streams.

9

"Your job is so easy."
said Mr. Bee to Ms. Mosquite.
"They can't even see you.
You're a sneak - you're a cheat!

At least I show my colors.
I am *proud*, I'm robust.
I boldly make my move
soon as I gain their trust."

"But that is cruel, that's mean!"
said Mosquite to Mr. Bee.
"But come to think of it
kinda reminds me... of me!

I too serve the moment at hand.
But I invisibly fly
and very quietly, I land."

They both hung in silence
mid-air, and stared.

And they thought about
the unfriendly jobs
they both shared.

"Wait!
Let's Google each other
and see if we do any good!

And maybe if we don't
well maybe we *should*."

"It says right here,"
BB said to Mosquito
"that you pollinate many plants
including the cocoa."

"So what you're saying
Mr. Bumble Bee
is that we wouldn't have chocolate
if not for mosquitoes like me?!"

"Ok now Skito,
don't go gettin' high fallutin'.
Google me now!
Let's get my horn a-tootin'!"

"Well, it says right here..."
Skito said to Mr. Buzzy.
Then she put on her glasses
cause the words looked kinda fuzzy.

"Our black and yellow friends
pollinate all the trees.
So there'd be no fruit
if it wasn't for the bees!"

The two were so relieved.
Their purpose wasn't just
stingin' and bitin'.
They make the world
what it is.
Then & there
they stopped their fightin'.

"People always say,
'Nothing's perfect.' "
The Mosquito said to the Bee.
"We're here to make sure
it stays that way."
They shook wings and stingers
and heartily agreed.

THANK YOU

To Eric Brown, my brother-in-law,
who upon reading this scribbled story
in my journal said quite directly,
"You should make a book out of this...
for real... you should." I think it's the fact that
he doesn't talk a lot that made that sentence
really stand out. Thank you to the Brown family
for inspiring me to be me. Also, for their
cozy house in Stowe, Vermont,
where this book was dreamed up.